# 26 MILES

## BY QUIARA ALEGRÍA HUDES

★

DRAMATISTS
PLAY SERVICE
INC.

26 MILES was originally commissioned and developed by South Coast Repertory (David Emmes, Producing Artistic Director; Martin Benson, Artistic Director) with support from the Elizabeth George Foundation. The play was further developed at Signature Theatre (Eric Schaeffer, Artistic Director) and Seattle Repertory (Jerry Manning, Producing Artistic Director; Benjamin Moore, Artistic Director)

The rolling world professional premieres of 26 MILES were funded through the National New Play Network (NNPN) Continued Life New Plays Fund (Jason Loewith, Executive Director). The first NNPN world premiere opened on March 20, 2009, at the Alliance Theatre in Atlanta (Susan Booth, Artistic Director). The second NNPN world premiere opened on May 9, 2009, at the Curious Theatre Company in Denver (Chip Walton, Producing Artistic Director). The third NNPN world premiere opened on November 19, 2009, at the New Theatre in Coral Gables, FL. (Ricky J. Martinez, Artistic Director).

## SPECIAL NOTE ON SONGS AND RECORDINGS

For performances of copyrighted songs, arrangements or recordings mentioned in this Play, the permission of the copyright owner(s) must be obtained. Other songs, arrangements or recordings may be substituted provided permission from the copyright owner(s) of such songs, arrangements or recordings is obtained; or songs, arrangements or recordings in the public domain may be substituted.

*For Ray, who brought me coffee.*

26 MILES received its world premiere at the Alliance Theatre in Atlanta, Georgia, on March 20, 2009. It was directed by Kent Gash; the set design was by Kat Conley; the costume design was by English Benning; the lighting design was by William H. Grant, III; the sound design was by Caly Benning; the projection design was by Adam Larsen; and the dramaturg was Celise Kalke. The cast was as follows:

OLIVIA ........................................................ Bethany Anne Lind
BEATRIZ ......................................................... Socorro Santiago
AARON ............................................................. Jason MacDonald
MANUEL ............................................................ Triney Sandoval

26 MILES received its second world premiere on May 9, 2009, at the Curious Theatre Company in Denver, Colorado. It was directed by Pesha Rudnick; the set design was by Michael R. Duran; the lighting design was by Richard Devin; the costume design was by Emilee Cooper; the sound design was by Brian Freeland; the dramaturg was Jennifer Fawcett; and the production stage manager was Kelly Johnson. The cast was as follows:
OLIVIA .................................................................. Ana Noguera
BEATRIZ ..................................................... Gabriella Cavallero
AARON ...................................................................... Kevin Hart
MANUEL .................................................. José Antonio Mercado

26 MILES received its third world premiere at the New Theatre in Coral Gables, Florida, opening on November 20, 2009. It was directed by Ricky J. Martinez; the set design was by Yamarys Salomon; the lighting design was by David Hernandez; the sound design was by Ozzie Quintana; and the costume coordinator and production stage manager was Dana Hesch. The cast was as follows:

OLIVIA ................................................................. Jackie Rivera
BEATRIZ ............................................................... Evelyn Perez
AARON ........................................................... Derek Warriner
MANUEL ................................................ Christopher Vicchiollo

# CHARACTERS

OLIVIA — 15, looks white

BEATRIZ — 40s, Cuban, dark skin (doubles as Janet)

AARON — 40s (doubles as Joe, Attendant, and Reader 2)

MANUEL — 40s (doubles as Tamál Seller, Uemura, and Reader 1)

# TIME

1986.

# SETTING

The play opens on two households: One in Paoli, a suburb of Philadelphia. The owners never put much attention into decorating; even things with color seem like oatmeal. A staircase leading to an upper floor is prominently featured. The second household, in Philadelphia, is a twin Victorian decorated with fine antiques.

Later, an exquisite antique chair from Philadelphia becomes the driver's seat of a car, and a rustic wooden chair from Paoli becomes the passenger's seat.

Finally, sky.

# 26 MILES

## Scene 1

*Paoli. Olivia, 15, wears ugly sweatpants. She holds a zine.*

OLIVIA.  September 1986, Volume 1, Number 6.
Dear Reader,
   Thank you for picking up the sixth issue of *The Issue.* You may notice that our format is not exactly glossy, that our printing is still black and white. Please, embrace the "poor-printing" aesthetic. The emphasis here is content, is questioning. *(An anonymous imaginary figure enters, reading a copy of* The Issue.*)*
   This month we look at thought experiments: elaborate what-ifs that help us understand the world we live in.
   Imagine people are divided into two groups: pickpockets and non-pickpockets. Pickpockets may only steal from other pickpockets; their wallets are stolen time and time again. Non-pickpockets keep the same wallet their entire life. Finally, you may choose which group you belong to.
   Imagine that one day an old pickpocket named Joe *(A pickpocket named Joe enters, in silhouette.)* is walking down the street and his hand slips into a nearby pocket and he pulls out a wallet that rings a bell in the back of his mind. *(Joe steals the reader's wallet.)*
   As Joe walks away, he realizes that what he holds in his hand is his very first original wallet, decades later. The leather is dry and crackly, there's a single dollar inside. It is the fossil of an earlier self.
   Joe walks home to his wife, Janet, a non-pickpocket. Her original wallet has never left her possession. It holds two credit cards and plenty of cash. The leather? Soft and supple. *(Janet pulls out her wallet. Joe and Janet look at their wallets.)*
   The question is, would you rather be Joe or Janet? Would you

part with your original wallet? Or keep it safely in your possession? If you said Janet, this magazine may not be for you. *(Janet exits. The reader realizes his wallet is stolen, exits.)*

    Dear Reader, what if these pages —

JOE. — reach eyes I've never seen?

OLIVIA. What if these words —

JOE. — travel places I've never been?

OLIVIA. Parentheses. I've been two places: Philadelphia and Paoli, a suburb of Philadelphia. End parentheses. Fellow pickpockets of the world, enjoy.

    Olivia Jacobs, Founding Editor-In-Chief.

## Scene 2

*Late at night. Olivia curls on the third step of the staircase holding a plastic bag. She shivers. She throws up into the bag.*

OLIVIA. *(Whispering.)* Dad? Dad? Dad … *(She throws up again. She climbs to the fourth step.)* Daddy … Dad … *(Aaron appears at the top of the staircase.)*

AARON. Olivia? Oh my God.

OLIVIA. Dad.

AARON. Have you been down here a long time?

OLIVIA. I was whispering. I didn't want …

AARON. Why didn't you come upstairs and wake me, honey?

OLIVIA. Deborah said …

AARON. Jesus.

OLIVIA. She said I'm not allowed on the third floor.

AARON. When did she say that?

OLIVIA. Last Chanukah.

AARON. Well, come up quietly and tap on my shoulder. Did you throw up?

OLIVIA. Thirteen times.

AARON. Oh, honey.

OLIVIA. I missed the toilet the first time. Sorry.

AARON. Olivia.

OLIVIA. I cleaned it up.

AARON. What's in the bag?

OLIVIA. It's disgusting.

AARON. You threw up in that? Put that in the trash, Jesus.

OLIVIA. Sorry. *(She exits.)*

AARON. *(Calling after her.)* Tie it tight! *(She reenters without the bag.)* You're covered in sweat.

OLIVIA. I'm so sorry, Dad. I'm sorry.

AARON. What are you sorry for? *(Pause.)* Honey, it's okay. Talk to me.

OLIVIA. I think it was dinner.

AARON. That's the last time we order from China Star. That broccoli with garlic sauce had some mysterious lumps. They say Chinese Food Syndrome can be lethal. *(Pause.)* What can I do? Tell me what to do.

OLIVIA. You tell me. You're supposed to know!

AARON. What's wrong, honey? *(No answer.)* I know I'm not doing the best job at things —

OLIVIA. I'm not allowed upstairs. I'm not allowed to talk about Mom.

AARON. *Please* don't listen to Deborah's rules.

OLIVIA. I needed to talk to you after school and I went upstairs and she yelled at me.

AARON. I could read to you. *National Geographic* came.

OLIVIA. Dad, I'm not eight anymore! *(Pause.)* Can I get a new pair of jeans? Like jean shorts or knickers?

AARON. Sure. You and Deborah can go to the mall this weekend.

OLIVIA. No. You take me.

AARON. I don't know anything about girls' clothes.

OLIVIA. Forget it. I'll just wear these ugly fucking sweatpants.

AARON. Olivia, for Christ's sake! Do you think I'm happy with this? You think this is how I wanted things to be?

OLIVIA. *(Pause.)* The new cabinet looks good. It's almost done.

AARON. *(Pause.)* Tomorrow I'm varnishing.

OLIVIA. Black walnut?

AARON. *(He nods.)* Could you tell what kind of joints I used?

OLIVIA. Mortise and tennon.

AARON. The drawers?

OLIVIA. Dovetail.

AARON. I was at the lumberyard today, I saw this band-milled pine. Perfect for a log cabin ...

OLIVIA. You and I are going to drive away from everything.

AARON. Build a cabin in the woods. Barbecue every night. Have a small wooden dock to dive from. Go digging for clams. / Set traps for crabs.

OLIVIA. *(Same time.)* Set traps for crabs.

AARON. Wyoming, right?

OLIVIA. Wyoming.

AARON. You always said that was the place to be.

OLIVIA. *(Pointed.)* So when do we leave? Tomorrow? *(Pause.)*

AARON. Deborah lost another one.

OLIVIA. When?

AARON. After the third one she decided to stop telling people.

OLIVIA. So this was miscarriage number...?

AARON. Six. She really wants a child of her own.

OLIVIA. *(Getting up.)* I should sleep.

AARON. *(As she goes.)* There's Pepto in the cabinet ... *(Olivia is gone. Aaron climbs back up the stairs. Lights rise opposite to a house in Philadelphia. Same time. Beatriz and Manuel are in bed. Manuel is reading a book, Beatriz wakes up.)*

BEATRIZ. What time is it, Papi?

MANUEL. Four-thirty.

BEATRIZ. Turn out the light.

MANUEL. I'm almost done with this chapter.

BEATRIZ. Close the book and go to sleep.

MANUEL. The Catholic Church lied to us hook, line, and sinker. And we fell for it.

BEATRIZ. *You* fell for it. Don't rope me into that obnoxious book.

MANUEL. I'm trying to expand my mind.

BEATRIZ. I'm trying to sleep.

MANUEL. God is a manmade invention.

BEATRIZ. *Ay, por favor!*

MANUEL. You think it's about heaven and hell? You think it's about Jesus's love? The Lamb of God? It's about manipulation of the public. It's about power.

BEATRIZ. I'm going to throw that book away. That thing has twisted your brain.

MANUEL. I'm telling you, *negra,* you want to know your history?

BEATRIZ. I know my history!

MANUEL. Why do you think the Catholic Church targeted the

Cubans? And the South Americans? Because we got the gold and we got the sugarcane!

BEATRIZ.   Your whole family is Catholics, you believe everything you're told to the letter. Whether it's the Bible or some hack historian.

MANUEL.   You think being Protestant makes you intellectual? Your father was a farmer, same as mine.

BEATRIZ.   Next month you'll read another book and you'll spout exactly what that one says. Even if it says a tree will sprout from your asshole. Even if it says, hey, that cockroach is a prophet! That turd on the sidewalk? That's the holy grail!

MANUEL.   There is no holy grail, *negra!*

BEATRIZ.   When I couldn't eat a bite of food. When I sat on the floor wishing lightning would split me in two like a rotten tree trunk! Who dragged me up?

MANUEL.   That has nothing to do with this.

BEATRIZ.   You looked me in the eye and told me to surrender. Surrender to what, Papi?

MANUEL.   That's in the past, *negra.*

BEATRIZ.   Surrender to God, Papi! So I'm taking all your books and I'm burning them!

MANUEL.   You don't touch my books!

BEATRIZ.   Go ahead, fall asleep, and I'm taking that paper menace and I'm putting it in the fireplace where it belongs!

MANUEL.   And then I'll burn your spiritual journals! I'll burn your tarot cards, I'll burn your altars! I will — *(The phone rings. Beatriz answers it.)*

BEATRIZ.   Hello? Hello? *(Pissed.)* Who is this? I can hear you breathing!

OLIVIA.   Mom? *(Lights rise in the suburbs. Olivia is on the staircase.)*

BEATRIZ.   *Mija?*

OLIVIA.   Mom, it's Olivia.

BEATRIZ.   I know who it is.

OLIVIA.   Well, it's been five months.

BEATRIZ.   *Niña,* what's wrong? *(No answer.)* Are you okay?

OLIVIA.   NO I'M NOT OKAY! Oh God, hold on … *(Olivia runs offstage, throws up.)*

BEATRIZ.   Olivia? *Niña!*

MANUEL.   What's going on?

BEATRIZ.   I can't take this. I can't live like this.

MANUEL. What it is, *negra?*

BEATRIZ. *Ay, dios mio.* How far can I bend? How far can I fucking bend? *(Olivia returns.)*

OLIVIA. Okay, sorry.

BEATRIZ. Where are you?

OLIVIA. At home.

BEATRIZ. Can you tell me what happened?

OLIVIA. I just wanted to hear your voice. Talk to me?

BEATRIZ. I can't hear you, *niña.*

OLIVIA. Everyone's asleep.

BEATRIZ. You sound like you've seen a ghost.

OLIVIA. I threw up fifteen times. I'm not even throwing up anymore, it's just spit coming out.

BEATRIZ. Was it something you ate?

OLIVIA. No.

BEATRIZ. *Coño,* is anyone taking care of you?

OLIVIA. Dad has work in the morning.

BEATRIZ. Is that woman there?

OLIVIA. She's asleep.

BEATRIZ. I'm coming to get you.

OLIVIA. No!

BEATRIZ. Pack a bag and wait by the door.

OLIVIA. Never mind. I shouldn't have called you!

BEATRIZ. Pack your fucking bags!

OLIVIA. Can't they arrest you?

BEATRIZ. Let them shoot me for all I care! You're my daughter and I can't live like this anymore, Olivia. *No puedo.*

MANUEL. *Negra, cálmate.*

OLIVIA. I should go ask Dad.

BEATRIZ. Excuse me, is your father sitting by your side?

OLIVIA. No.

BEATRIZ. Did that man hold your hair back while you vomited? Did he put a towel on the bathroom floor so your knees wouldn't get cold?

OLIVIA. My knees are freezing.

BEATRIZ. Could he even be bothered to bring you a glass of water?

OLIVIA. I'm so thirsty, Mom.

BEATRIZ. Then fuck him! Give me an hour. I'll honk twice. You run out.

OLIVIA. Don't make a scene. Just tap lightly on the door.

14

BEATRIZ. Excuse me, I am not touching that woman's property. What's the address again?

OLIVIA. 65 Carol Lane. Ugh, I think number sixteen's coming on ... *(Olivia drops the phone and runs to the bathroom.)*

BEATRIZ. Olivia! *(She hangs up.)* Ay, Jesús, stop me from doing something crazy. I'm about to do something I'll regret.

MANUEL. *Negra*, what's going on?

BEATRIZ. She's puking her guts out and her father's in bed having sweet dreams!

MANUEL. I'm coming with you.

BEATRIZ. Let me handle this, Papi. I don't need anyone else's bullshit right now. Just read your book and call Susan McPhee.

MANUEL. *(Taken aback.)* What?

BEATRIZ. Where's the keys?

MANUEL. In my pants pocket ... Do you want coffee?

BEATRIZ. Make up a bed for Olivia. I'll be back soon.

MANUEL. The car needs gas.

BEATRIZ. The Lord works in mysterious ways, Papi. You told me, surrender, and the Lord will make things right. And guess what? Ten years later, and you delivered on your promise. So thank you, Papi. Thank you. *(She finds the car keys and exits.)*


## Scene 3


*Two horn honks. Lights barely rise to Paoli. Beatriz stands at the foot of the Jacobs' driveway.*


BEATRIZ. Olivia! *(A dog barks.)* Olivia! *Vamos*, the car is still running! Olivia! *Ay dios mio.* Aaron! Deborah! I know you can hear me! You're not deaf! Give me my daughter! I want my daughter! Olivia! *(A screen door slams shut.)* What are you looking at? You never seen a crazy Cuban bitch before? *(The screen door slams shut again.)* Olivia! *Ay dios mio.* Aaron! Hey! I saw you peeking out that curtain! You don't know how to care for a sick child? Send Olivia out to me! Send me my baby! I'm taking her! I'm taking my daughter from you and that evil witch! Olivia! *(Calming herself.)*

*Padre nuestro que estás en los cielos, santificado sea tu nombre ...*
*Mundo sin fin. Mundo sin fin. (Olivia appears with a backpack.)*

OLIVIA. Mom? I told you to be quiet.

BEATRIZ. You're okay. My baby's okay. Ay, thank God. *Gracias a dios. Que dios te bendiga. Que dios te cuide. Mi niña. Mi hija sagrada.*

OLIVIA. I said don't make a scene.

BEATRIZ. You could have passed out for all I knew.

OLIVIA. What are we going to do?

BEATRIZ. Are you still vomiting? Should we go to the hospital?

OLIVIA. Number sixteen felt like the end.

BEATRIZ. I brought plastic bags just in case. Tomorrow we'll go to the doctor.

OLIVIA. I brought a change of clothes and my magazines.

BEATRIZ. I am never letting you go again.

OLIVIA. I almost forgot my good luck charm. *(Olivia shows a folded up magazine page. She puts it in her pocket.)*

BEATRIZ. They're lucky I don't have a gun. I was about to go in that house and start shooting.

OLIVIA. Oh crap. The kitchen light is on. They're awake.

BEATRIZ. Good. You know what? *(She shouts.)* FUCK THEM!!!

OLIVIA. Oh, crap, the hallway light! Let's go! *(They exit.)*


# Scene 4


*Afternoon. A convenience store and gas station. Beatriz is at the counter.*


BEATRIZ. Twenty dollars on pump seven. And one of those road maps.

ATTENDANT. Bad day to be out on the road.

BEATRIZ. I had to pull over twice. But the rain's letting up.

ATTENDANT. That's twenty-six eighteen.

BEATRIZ. Do you take AmEx? *(Pause.)* American Express.

ATTENDANT. You're not from around here.

BEATRIZ. Philadelphia.

ATTENDANT. Cheese steaks.

16

BEATRIZ. Ugh. I can't eat that junk anymore.

ATTENDANT. Liberty Bell. Got that big crack up the side. I got an uncle in South Philly, a butcher.

BEATRIZ. Hollywood Meat Market?

ATTENDANT. No kidding!

BEATRIZ. That's where I get my Thanksgiving turkey, every year.

ATTENDANT. Small world.

BEATRIZ. Do you know, are there any good antique stores in the area?

ATTENDANT. My mom's into all that old stuff. Old teddy bears and dolls. Spends her entire check. Baby faces without eyes. Gives me the creeps.

BEATRIZ. For me it's doorknobs. Hinges. Sconces. Fixtures. Jewelry for the house.

ATTENDANT. Try King's over on Main. *(Olivia enters, sleepy.)*

OLIVIA. Morning. Ugh, my neck.

BEATRIZ. Hey. How are you feeling, *niña?*

OLIVIA. I can't believe the sun's out. I slept.

BEATRIZ. You snored.

OLIVIA. Really?

BEATRIZ. Like a grizzly bear.

OLIVIA. Sorry.

BEATRIZ. Please. It was music to my ears.

OLIVIA. I'm ravenous. My stomach feels like a black hole.

BEATRIZ. Your choice. Banana or granola bar. Then we'll go find a real lunch.

OLIVIA. Banana. *(She takes a banana.)* I'm so confused. What time is it?

BEATRIZ. I left my watch in the car.

ATTENDANT. Just past four.

OLIVIA. Whoa ... What part of Philly is this?

ATTENDANT. Hon, this ain't Filth-adelphia.

BEATRIZ. I got a road map. You be my navigator. *(Hands her a map.)*

OLIVIA. Did you get lost?

BEATRIZ. Sort of.

OLIVIA. Where are we?

BEATRIZ. Lima. *(Pronounced "lee-ma.")*

ATTENDANT. Lima. *(Pronounced "lie-ma.")*

BEATRIZ. Lima? Oh, man! You've got to be kidding me.

ATTENDANT. Like the bean.

OLIVIA. And where's Lima?

ATTENDANT. Ohio.

OLIVIA. Ohio state?!

BEATRIZ. I just drove. I just kept driving.

OLIVIA. Oh my God.

BEATRIZ. You were sound asleep back there. I didn't want to wake you.

OLIVIA. Are you crazy?

BEATRIZ. I haven't heard you snore like that since you were six.

OLIVIA. What are you, kidnapping me?

BEATRIZ. My foot wouldn't come off the gas pedal.

OLIVIA. Dad's going to kill me. He was right.

BEATRIZ. What?

OLIVIA. Nothing.

BEATRIZ. What did he say about me?

OLIVIA. You're irrational.

BEATRIZ. I … I thought maybe we could take a trip. Drive. Talk. Get to know each other.

OLIVIA. I left him a note saying I'd be back on Monday.

BEATRIZ. Well, a short trip.

OLIVIA. He could call the cops.

ATTENDANT. Excuse me, is there some illegal activity going on here? *(To Olivia.)* Do you know this woman?

OLIVIA. She's my mom.

ATTENDANT. Your biological mother?

BEATRIZ. I'm her mother.

OLIVIA. She just doesn't have custody of me.

BEATRIZ. Olivia. Shut it.

OLIVIA. She has no visitation rights. *(Pause. Beatriz slams some cash on the counter.)*

BEATRIZ. Twenty on pump seven. *(To Olivia.)* I'll have you back to your father in no time. *(She exits.)*

OLIVIA. Mom! Shit.

# Scene 5

*The gas pump. Olivia approaches Beatriz.*


BEATRIZ. *(Upset.)* Vamos. Did you use the bathroom?

OLIVIA. The guy said there's a diner on Main Street.

BEATRIZ. Forget it. We're turning around. I don't know what I was thinking.

OLIVIA. He said they've got the best milkshakes in town.

BEATRIZ. I'm not hungry, Olivia!

OLIVIA. I'm sorry, Mom.

BEATRIZ. Don't go telling people my private business.

OLIVIA. *(An apology.)* As soon as the words came out ...

BEATRIZ. I'm your mother. Don't apologize for me. Don't explain me. *(Pause.)*

OLIVIA. If you could go anywhere in the world, where would it be?

BEATRIZ. *Ay, niña, métete en el jodío carro!*

OLIVIA. *(Not understanding the Spanish.)* What?

BEATRIZ. I said, "Get in the fucking car."

OLIVIA. If you could go anywhere in the world, Mom—

BEATRIZ. I'd go far away. I'd go back to Cuba when I was twelve Baracoa had a big flood that year. It wiped out our farm. But up until then, it was beautiful.

OLIVIA. Badicoa ...

BEATRIZ. *(Correcting her.)* Baracoa.

OLIVIA. *(Slowly.)* Baracoa. *(Olivia hands her a state map.)*

BEATRIZ. Wyoming?

OLIVIA. Two bucks. Not bad for a state map.

BEATRIZ. What's in Wyoming?

OLIVIA. Stuff that's not in Paoli.

# Scene 6

*Main Street. Olivia sits on a bench, writing quickly, excited.*

OLIVIA. Dear Reader, *(Two anonymous readers enter, rapt in the pages of* The Issue.*)* Lewis and Clark, Jack Kerouac, and me: hitting the road! Parentheses. With biological mother, haven't lived with in eight years, last time I saw her was Grandma's funeral. End parentheses. Thank you for picking up seventh *Issue*, writing in shorthand so forgive grammar, apologies for delay in production, due to circumstances no way I'll be publishing on time this month. No reference books or research materials, no typewriter so no 108 words per minute, Bic pen and spiral notepad only, can't read own writing, terrible penmanship, left hand cramping. The theme of this issue will be …

READER 1. *(A suggestion.)* Flight?

OLIVIA. Yes.

READER 2. Getaway.

READER 1. Discovery.

OLIVIA. Are the days of great explorers over? Has every corner of this country been tagged, examined, catalogued? If I stumble upon said discovery will I even know? Darwin was aboard the *Beagle* five years didn't fully realize his theory until thirty years later.

READER 2. Detailed field notes important.

READER 1. Could fuel life's work.

OLIVIA. *(Pause.)* She's pretty. I have these spiderweb brows, she has these Frida Kahlo jungles over her eyes. *(A horn honk.)* Ahh!

# Scene 7

*The open road. A car. There are shopping bags in the back seat.*

BEATRIZ.  Who would have guessed? Lima, Ohio has kick-ass antiques! *Carajo,* she had this stepback cupboard, original Shaker period. And she only wanted four-fifty! You know how much I could resell that for?

OLIVIA.  You should have bought it.

BEATRIZ.  One piece per store, that's my rule. Anyhow, it wouldn't fit in the back seat. So, show me, show me!

OLIVIA.  *(Pulls books out of a bag.)* Well, I found … *Around the Globe,* a survey of important explorers over the last two thousand years. And *Basic North American Geology.*

BEATRIZ.  There should be one more in there. I bought it while you weren't looking.

OLIVIA.  *(Pulls out another book.) Changing Bodies, Changing Lives?*

BEATRIZ.  There's an excellent chapter on birth control.

OLIVIA.  They teach sex ed at my school.

BEATRIZ.  Read the chapter, then you and I are going to have a talk.

OLIVIA.  *(Points.)* 80 West, left lane.

BEATRIZ.  Okay, look in my bag. *(Olivia pulls a glass doorknob out of a bag.)* Chinese porcelain. They don't make 'em like that anymore. That's for the third floor, for your bathroom.

OLIVIA.  I have a bathroom at your house?

BEATRIZ.  Someone made that by hand. Original brass doorplate.

OLIVIA.  Do you usually go 45 on the highway?

BEATRIZ.  I'm trying not to get pulled over. One look, people know I'm not from these parts.

OLIVIA.  Come on, use the gas. Drive.

BEATRIZ.  *Maneja.*

OLIVIA.  What's that?

BEATRIZ.  *Drive* in Spanish.

OLIVIA.  *Maneja. (Olivia pulls out her notebook, writes.)* M-A-N?

BEATRIZ.  *Ay dios mio,* don't write it, just remember the sounds!

OLIVIA.  *(Closes the notebook.)* Teach me five Spanish words a day?

BEATRIZ. *Ventana.*
OLIVIA. Window?
BEATRIZ. *Baja la ventana.*
OLIVIA. Open the window?
BEATRIZ. *Perfecto! (Olivia rolls down the window.)*
OLIVIA. You too. Open your window all the way. *Maneja!*
*(Beatriz rolls down the window. Their hair blows in the wind.)*
Ahhhh! The air!
BEATRIZ. Rain finally let up!
OLIVIA. Like the road was built for us.
BEATRIZ. Let's go find us some mountains! Tall ones, with evergreens at the bottom and snow on the top!
OLIVIA. Are we going to cross the Mississippi? We gotta drive over some suspension bridges!
BEATRIZ. Waterfalls! I love waterfalls.
OLIVIA. Canyons!
BEATRIZ. Sand dunes!
OLIVIA. Train tracks and main streets!
BEATRIZ. Where's Route 66?
OLIVIA. Where's Vegas?
BEATRIZ. We'll honk at anyone going slower than fifty-five! *(She honks the horn.) Muévete, coño!*
OLIVIA. No one was there!
BEATRIZ. Practice! We got places to go!
OLIVIA. Most importantly, we'll see the buffalo.
BEATRIZ. Trace the airways of bald eagles!
OLIVIA. Right, but buffalo first.
BEATRIZ. We'll chase down wild turkeys!
OLIVIA. No. We have to see a buffalo. That's what's in Wyoming. We have to see one.
BEATRIZ. Buffalo it is.
OLIVIA. Yellowstone Park. You drive to Hayden Valley and watch them run.
BEATRIZ. You've been there before?
OLIVIA. In my first ever *National Geographic*, there was this photograph. A mountain covered in snow. And one single buffalo running, like a dark brown iris on a white white eye. I thought, all this schooling and I finally *know* something. I need to see a buffalo run in the snow.
BEATRIZ. You just knew.

OLIVIA.  The second I saw it.

BEATRIZ.  But it's September. There's not going to be snow in Wyoming.

OLIVIA.  *(Pause.)* Still. The important thing is the running. It's not about the snow. It's feeling the ground shake. Hearing the sound of the hooves. In the photograph, he was completely airborne, none of his hooves were touching the ground. Like he was flying. And I thought, I need to feel the rhythm, the earth shaking. It's the only way I'll believe his feet ever touch the ground. *(Olivia pulls a folded-up magazine page out of her pocket.)* Look.

BEATRIZ.  Not while I'm driving.


# Scene 8


*Sunset. A diner parking lot. Two adjoining payphones. Manuel and Beatriz on the phone.*


MANUEL.  *Negra,* I have a dentist appointment in Conshohocken

BEATRIZ.  Reschedule it. They're always rescheduling on you.

MANUEL.  My back tooth is killing me.

BEATRIZ.  There's ibuprofen in the cabinet.

MANUEL.  I have to be at the glass distributor first thing in the morning.

BEATRIZ.  Have your brother take you.

MANUEL.  All those supplies aren't going to fit in Tom's car. His car is a piece of shit!

BEATRIZ.  Then call a taxi.

MANUEL.  I don't take taxis!

BEATRIZ.  Go rent that truck you want to buy, see if you like it.

MANUEL.  *Negra.* I had to cancel the meeting with License and Inspection this morning. You're supposed to meet with the unions on Thursday.

BEATRIZ.  Well, you know what, figure it out on your own.

MANUEL.  Don't expect me to meet with no unions! What about the bills?

BEATRIZ.  You pay them this month. Be your own secretary.

MANUEL. Where's the checkbook?

BEATRIZ. While you're at it, take a good hard look at the phone bill. Those calls aren't free, Papi.

MANUEL. *(Pause.)* Is Olivia okay?

BEATRIZ. *(What's really on her mind.)* Where were you on Thursday? I waited outside the doctor's for an hour.

MANUEL. What did he say?

BEATRIZ. Just pay the phone bill. Don't worry about me.

MANUEL. What did he say, *negra? (No answer.)* I started a new book.

BEATRIZ. *Ay,* Papi, I'm not in the mood to be educated!

MANUEL. *Twelve Steps to Forgiveness.* When you get back, I want you to read it.

BEATRIZ. When I get back? *Viejo,* you don't hear a word I say, do you?

MANUEL. Hello? *Negra?*

BEATRIZ. I'm all out of quarters.

MANUEL. Twenty-five cents. The lady's saying twenty-five cents!

BEATRIZ. I'm in Indiana. The call's expensive.

MANUEL. Indiana? *(They get disconnected. Beatriz crumples, cries. Olivia takes her turn on the phone. She dials a number, waits.)*

OLIVIA. Hey Dad, it's me. Again. I didn't mean to take off like that. Don't be mad, okay? I'm just on a brief spontaneous vacation with Mom. It's a loose itinerary so I don't know exactly when I'll be back, but soon, I promise. I called Allison to get my homework. When we get to the next motel I'll try you again. Driving reminds me of you 'cuz we always said how — hello? No way, that was like twenty seconds! Where's my quarters? Quarters! Hello? Hello? Aw, shit! *(Olivia hangs up, approaches Beatriz.)* You ready?

BEATRIZ. That was quick. No luck?

OLIVIA. I caught him on the way out the door.

BEATRIZ. Everything okay?

OLIVIA. *(A bad liar.)* He misses me. How's Manuel?

BEATRIZ. *(Also a bad liar.)* He says hello.

# Scene 9

*The open road. Olivia is looking through cassette tapes.*

OLIVIA.  The blue tape?

BEATRIZ.  The white one.

OLIVIA.  Side A or B?

BEATRIZ.  A. *(Olivia puts a tape in. Gloria Estefan's "Conga"
plays.\*)* Wepa!

OLIVIA.  Oh God.

BEATRIZ.  What?

OLIVIA.  They play this song fifty times a day.

BEATRIZ.  The first time I heard this, I was on the expressway, my
heart literally stopped. My whole body started shaking. I had to
pull over onto the shoulder. I was like, holy shit, this is going to be
the next cultural evolution! The last person to touch any of this was
Santana. And now we got a woman doing it!

OLIVIA.  Okay, mind if I turn it down?

BEATRIZ.  What kind of music do you like?

OLIVIA.  Chopin *Nocturnes.*

BEATRIZ.  I mean, what kind of music do you shake your ass to?

OLIVIA.  What ass?

BEATRIZ.  The one you're sitting on.

OLIVIA.  My ass is flat as the highway. Not made for shaking.

BEATRIZ.  You're my daughter, you have a spiritual ass.

OLIVIA.  *(Turns off the music.)* Sorry, I get carsick.

BEATRIZ.  So tell me about life in eighth grade.

OLIVIA.  Tenth grade.

BEATRIZ.  That's what I meant.

OLIVIA.  I'm in high school.

BEATRIZ.  *(Pause.)* What's your boyfriend's name?

OLIVIA.  What boyfriend?

BEATRIZ.  Who have you been kissing, huh?

OLIVIA.  No one lately.

BEATRIZ.  When was your first time?

OLIVIA.  Ew! I'm a virgin!

BEATRIZ. Don't lie to me!

OLIVIA. When did you? For the first time?

BEATRIZ. Things were different then. Not so many diseases going around.

OLIVIA. So you were young!

BEATRIZ. No.

OLIVIA. Admit it. Naughty momma!

BEATRIZ. Ay. I wish I could tell you I lost my virginity on my wedding night. But since I never had a wedding night ...

OLIVIA. What do you mean?

BEATRIZ. Your father didn't believe in marriage.

OLIVIA. How'd you convince him?

BEATRIZ. I didn't. We lived in sin.

OLIVIA. Wait ...

BEATRIZ. Eleven years I slept in your father's bed and he didn't respect me enough to —

OLIVIA. I'm a bastard?

BEATRIZ. Eleven years.

OLIVIA. I'm a bastard!

BEATRIZ. He walked out on me and six months later he was married to Deborah. A diamond ring, a white dress.

OLIVIA. Can we ban her name from the car?

BEATRIZ. Grab your pen. *(Olivia grabs a pen.)* Write her name.

OLIVIA. *(Writing.)* Deborah ...

BEATRIZ. Her full name.

OLIVIA. Maiden or married?

BEATRIZ. Married.

OLIVIA. Deborah Jacobs.

BEATRIZ. Give me the paper. *(Beatriz kisses the paper ceremoniously, then throws it out the window. It spirals behind them.)*

OLIVIA. That was mean.

BEATRIZ. Why are you smiling?

OLIVIA. Doesn't make it right.

BEATRIZ. *Ay,* please! Take matters into your own hands. You want to learn five Spanish words a day? Here's one. *Cojones.* It's time you grow some!

OLIVIA. So ... how old were you ... when ...

BEATRIZ. Fifteen.

---

* See Special Note on Songs and Recordings on copyright page.

OLIVIA. That's not so young. A respectable age.

BEATRIZ. I oughta kick your ass!

OLIVIA. Who was your first?

BEATRIZ. Some hippie from a commune in West Philadelphia. He looked just like the Moody Blues singer. Blonde hair. *(Sings.)* "Nights in white satin ... Never reaching the end ... "

OLIVIA. What was his name?

BEATRIZ. Ron.

OLIVIA. Where?

BEATRIZ. In the back of a church.

OLIVIA. Ahhhhhh! Did it feel good?

BEATRIZ. The first time never feels good.

OLIVIA. Does it get better?

BEATRIZ. Yes. Then it gets bad again. It was just a few months after I came from Cuba. I wore thick black eyeliner. Platform shoes. I took my mother's iron and flattened my hair straight as the highway. On the same board she ironed my school uniform on. Though occasionally I wore my hair out like an afro.

OLIVIA. You can grow an afro?

BEATRIZ. I was the hottest thing in Philadelphia. Skinny as a stick. But with an ass ...

OLIVIA. Yet somehow I end up with stringy hair and no ass.

BEATRIZ. I had a big 'fro the day I met your father.

OLIVIA. Tell me!

BEATRIZ. He had a braid down to his ass crack!

OLIVIA. Dad had long hair?

BEATRIZ. Bushy sideburns ...

OLIVIA. Mr. Suburbia?!

BEATRIZ. It was Woodstock.

OLIVIA. What?! I thought Woodstock was an urban legend!

BEATRIZ. I was sixteen, I could barely speak English. Rittenhouse Square was the big hangout. My friend Kat pulled up in her van and was like, "Hop in. We're going to a concert." She didn't say it was a three-day-long concert. We turned onto the highway, I saw the city disappear behind me and I started to flip out. I was the baby, I knew Mami would have the police combing the streets for me! Four days later I get back to Philly caked in mud head to toe. She beat my ass blue with my three-inch platforms. But I didn't care. I was in looooove.

OLIVIA. What band was playing when you met?

BEATRIZ. Joe Cocker had just finished. Or ... Santana was tuning up?

OLIVIA. Were you stoned?

BEATRIZ. I smoked a joint *one time*. Your father was king of the potheads!

OLIVIA. What was the first thing you said to Dad?

BEATRIZ. *(Not remembering.) Ay dios mio!*

OLIVIA. Details, Mom!

BEATRIZ. He had just returned from Brussels. He was riding his motorcycle across Germany. A classy, handsome rebel. He fell head over heels for me.

OLIVIA. I can't imagine the two of you.

BEATRIZ. Everyone said we'd be together to the grave. I was a different person then. The Beatriz he knew? She's gone. She disappeared a long time ago.

OLIVIA. What happened to her? *(Beatriz doesn't answer.)*

## Scene 10

*Evening, a motel. Olivia sits on the bed, taking dictation in her notebook. Beatriz brushes her teeth, giving dictation.*

BEATRIZ. *(Animated, having a great time.)* ... Because I don't know how your mother raised you, but mine taught me to have respect for human beings, a concept you clearly don't understand!

OLIVIA. *(Writing, fast.)* Yeah! Hold on ... "Concept ... clearly ... understand ... "

BEATRIZ. *(Dictating.)* So *muchísimas gracias* for demonstrating why I'll never be shopping at one of your "fine" antique stores again. I will happily take my American Express to a place where they know who their valuable customers are. Have a blessed day and live in the everlasting light of Christ. Beatriz Cruz Torres! *(Done dictating.)*

OLIVIA. Awesome! Should I see if they have stamps at the front desk?

BEATRIZ. Now ... *(Exhales loudly.)* You can throw it away.

OLIVIA. Throw what away?

BEATRIZ. The letter.

OLIVIA. Excuse me?

BEATRIZ. It's not my job to educate anyone. Ignorance is a choice, that store manager made his bed, he can sleep in it.

OLIVIA. He asked you for three forms of ID. He didn't ask the white lady for one!

BEATRIZ. Bury it or it'll bury you. *(Sits on the bed, prays.)* Padre, hijo, y spiritu santo ... Lord, you have put ignorant asses into this world. Give me patience in dealing with them. *(Pause.)* And give me guidance in dealing with Manuel, *por favor.* *(To Olivia.)* You want to add anything?

OLIVIA. *(Suddenly uncomfortable.)* That's alright.

BEATRIZ. It doesn't have to be out loud. You can just say it in your head.

OLIVIA. *(Trapped.)* I'm. I'm taking notes on geology.

BEATRIZ. Amen. *(Pause.)* Do you believe in God?

OLIVIA. *(Extremely uncomfortable.)* No one ever just asked me like that.

BEATRIZ. Do you pray?

OLIVIA. What's the technical definition of prayer?

BEATRIZ. Opening your heart to the Creator, having a conversation from the soul.

OLIVIA. I write.

BEATRIZ. *(Pause.)* Do me a favor. In my purse there's a CVS bag. Open it for me.

OLIVIA. *(Finds a purse, pulls a box out of a plastic bag.)* "Easy to read plus/minus system. Results in less than a minute." Hold on. How long have you had this?

BEATRIZ. There was a pharmacy next to the gas station.

OLIVIA. You could've just asked me.

BEATRIZ. Why were you throwing up, Olivia?

OLIVIA. I'm not pregnant.

BEATRIZ. Why were you carsick yesterday?

OLIVIA. Because you pump the brakes.

BEATRIZ. Take the test and leave the bathroom door open.

OLIVIA. What?! No!

BEATRIZ. I have to see you actually pee on it. *(Olivia exits into the bathroom. Beatriz watches her. Sound of peeing.)*

OLIVIA. *(Offstage.)* Are you gonna watch me wipe, too? *(Beatriz*

29

*stops watching her, walks away.)*

BEATRIZ. *Padre, hijo, y spiritu santo* … This is the one thing I ask of you. I take back everything I asked for a minute ago. She's just a kid. *(Crosses herself. Calls out.)* Anything yet? *(No answer. Opens Olivia's notebook, reads.)* "Frida Kahlo jungles over her eyes … " *(The toilet flushes. Beatriz quickly closes the journal. Olivia reenters, throws the pregnancy test at her mom.)*

OLIVIA. Happy? Can I go to sleep now?

BEATRIZ. This is what mothers do, *mija.*

OLIVIA. Good night. *(She turns off the light.)*


## Scene 11


*The motel room, later that night. Olivia's sexy dream. A song like Joe Cocker's "With A Little Help from My Friends" or another rock ballad from Woodstock plays.\* Beatriz rises from her sleep. Aaron enters. Starting with her hand, he gives her little kisses all the way up her arm until he's finally at her lips. Olivia sits up in bed, watching.*


BEATRIZ. Brussels.

AARON. I ate Belgian chocolate in the Grande Palace.

BEATRIZ. You've been to Amsterdam.

AARON. Smoked pot while Jimi Hendrix blew out a speaker at the Gala du Disque.

BEATRIZ. Kyoto?

AARON. Sent paper boats sailing down the Okazaki Canal.

BEATRIZ. What do the Alps smell like?

AARON. A woman's hair. I slalomed down the Himalayas. The snow is smooth as the inside of your elbow.

BEATRIZ. Sri Lanka. India.

AARON. Rode my motorcycle from the Taj Mahal all the way to tea plantations in Kandy.

BEATRIZ. Cuba.

AARON. *(Sexy.)* I've never been to Cuba … *(They kiss. The music swells to a crescendo. Olivia watches.)*

# Scene 12

*A switchback road in the mountains. Dense white fog surrounds the car.*

BEATRIZ. You either know where we are or you don't!
OLIVIA. I'm telling you, it's not on the map!
BEATRIZ. I'm driving in a goddamn cloud!
OLIVIA. Wait, shit, I think that was our turn-off!
BEATRIZ. I can't see the front of the car!
OLIVIA. We just keep getting further — ugh, I can't read this while we drive. Pull over!
BEATRIZ. Off the side of the mountain? Find me my glasses.
OLIVIA. *(Throwing the map down.)* I give up!
BEATRIZ. My glasses, Olivia!
OLIVIA. Here!
BEATRIZ. *(Putting them on.)* I still can't see for shit!
OLIVIA. This fog has eyes and it's scowling at us. It's saying, "Stop, turn around. Go back from whence you came!" *(Pause.)* There! A gas station! Turn! *(Beatriz stops the car. A payphone and gas station sign are barely visible.)*
BEATRIZ. It's closed.
OLIVIA. We need directions!
BEATRIZ. Ohhhh, I'm about to pee on myself!
OLIVIA. *(Walking toward a payphone.)* I'm calling Dad.
BEATRIZ. Leave him alone, you're harassing him! *Ay,* I can't hold it in. I'll piss in the goddamn bushes!
OLIVIA. *(Puts a quarter in.)* That's real classy!
BEATRIZ. No one will see! *(Beatriz disappears into the fog.)*
OLIVIA. *(Into the phone.)* Hello, Dad? This is message number thirteen. Pick up the phone. It's Sunday, I know you're not working. *(Pause.)* Change the timer because the tape keeps cutting me off. The button's underneath, by the jack. *(Pause.)* Change the message

* See Special Note on Songs and Recordings on copyright page.

31

to your voice so at least I can hear it. *(She hangs up.)* Mom?
BEATRIZ. *(Unseen.)* Give me a second!
OLIVIA. Take your time. It's not like we're getting anywhere. *(A figure comes into view. It is a tamál seller. He bumps into Olivia.)* Oh crap!
TAMÁL SELLER. *Ay! Lo siento, perdón.*
OLIVIA. Oh my God, my heart almost leapt out of my ribcage.
TAMÁL SELLER. Tamál? *Dos por un dolar.*
OLIVIA. Uh, no. Thanks.
TAMÁL SELLER. *Tienes hambre?* Hungry?
OLIVIA. *No hambre.*
TAMÁL SELLER. No place to eat for many miles. *Dos por un dolar.*
OLIVIA. I heard you. No money. No dollars, okay? *(Calling out.)* Mom?
BEATRIZ. *(Unseen.) Niña espera!*
TAMÁL SELLER. Where you coming from?
OLIVIA. *Soy de* Paoli.
TAMÁL SELLER. They are speaking Spanish in Paoli?
OLIVIA. Definitely not.
TAMÁL SELLER. You are studying Spanish in school?
OLIVIA. *Mi madre es Cubana.*
TAMÁL SELLER. Ah. She is teaching you a little bit. Accent is good.
OLIVIA. Five words a day. *Cinco palabras* each *día.*
BEATRIZ. *(Appearing.)* Ay, I feel so much better. I'm a new woman. *(To Tamál Seller.)* Oh. *Buenos días.*
TAMÁL SELLER. *Buenos días.*
OLIVIA. *(To Beatriz.)* Do you have a dollar?
BEATRIZ. *(To Tamál Seller.) Chacho*, it smells great!
TAMÁL SELLER. Tamales. My wife is making them this morning. *Dos por un dolar.*
BEATRIZ. *Bueno, dame dos. (He gives her two tamales.)* Were you speaking Spanish?
OLIVIA. No.
TAMÁL SELLER. *Sí.* She is speaking a little bit.
BEATRIZ. *(Takes her first bite.)* Oh my God.
TAMÁL SELLER. It is okay?
BEATRIZ. It reminds me of a dish my mother used to make, when I was twelve. *Pastelitos.* You know what this tastes like? The mountain.

TAMÁL SELLER. Ah, you coming from the mountains.

BEATRIZ. *Sí, en Cuba.*

TAMÁL SELLER. We are coming from *las montañas de* Peru. Now we are living *en las montañas de* South Dakota.

BEATRIZ. *(Another bite.) Ay que rico! Hay un sabor de las montañas ...*

TAMÁL SELLER. *Claro, que si.*

OLIVIA. Hold on. What?

TAMÁL SELLER. That there is a specific flavor. There is a way that mountains taste.

BEATRIZ. Your wife has a very special touch.

TAMÁL SELLER. Ramona. But we call her Moncha. My little Moncha. Monchita. All night, Monchita is in the kitchen with the cornmeal, stirring the meat. She is putting inside meat, tomato. *como se dice "comino"?*

BEATRIZ. Cumin.

TAMÁL SELLER. Cumin, salt, *aceituna—*

OLIVIA. *Aceituna?*

BEATRIZ. Olives.

TAMÁL SELLER. Pimiento, many things. I am falling asleep, the sound of the pot, the sound of the metal spoon on wooden board, sound of her fingers with the cornmeal, sound of olive oil in the frying pan. I am falling asleep, boiling tomato sauce in my nose, smell of olive juice, smell of her armpits in the sweaty kitchen, smell of her hair in the kitchen, smell of banana leaves, smell of her thumbs pressing the meat into the center, smell of the cotton string she is wrapping around the banana leaf, smell of beef separating into stew, smell of sweet onion, smell of her tears because she is crying from sweet onion. Then I wake up and — tamales. *(He disappears into the fog. The women eat in silence. Beatriz finishes her tamál and starts to cry.)*

OLIVIA. What are you thinking about?

BEATRIZ. I only bought two tamales.

OLIVIA. Here. *(She hands Beatriz the rest of her tamál.)*

BEATRIZ. Most cookbooks are like math. One spoon this, two spoons that. Bake the loaf. That's the only true recipe I've ever heard. *(Pause.)* No man has ever loved me like that.

# Scene 13

*A motel room. Sounds of a shower. Beatriz is on the phone.*

BEATRIZ.  Aaron? I know you're there. Pick up the phone before I leave a message for both you and Deborah to enjoy. *(Lights up in Paoli. Aaron picks up the phone.)*
AARON.  Hi, Beatriz.
BEATRIZ.  Surprise, surprise.
AARON.  Sorry I've been hard to track down …
BEATRIZ.  She's been trying to get in touch with you.
AARON.  I know, BB.
BEATRIZ.  Beatriz, not BB.
AARON.  I've been putting in a roof and one of my guys got the flu …
BEATRIZ.  What's going on, Aaron? She called you fifty times.
AARON.  Don't exaggerate.
BEATRIZ.  At least twice a day.
AARON.  Is she okay?
BEATRIZ.  You've had her for eight years, you tell me!
AARON.  She gets really quiet sometimes.
BEATRIZ.  Actually she has a lot to say. The girl's a philosopher. She's a poet.
AARON.  She's private about her writing and I respect her space.
BEATRIZ.  Space? She's fifteen! She doesn't need space! I looked in her notebook when she was sleeping.
AARON.  Some things never change.
BEATRIZ.  Damn straight!
AARON.  *(Curious.)* What did you read?
BEATRIZ.  *(Warm.)* She's an intellectual, same as you. I mean, the thoughts that go through her head. I can't believe a fifteen-year-old can think up this stuff.
AARON.  I wish she would show me.
BEATRIZ.  Essays trying to connect all these disconnected things. Like the national highway system with coincidence and luck. She makes chaos make sense. Like connecting the geography

34

of canyons with … with sadness.

AARON. *Geology* of canyons?

BEATRIZ. I know English, Aaron. You don't have to correct me.

AARON. No, I just … Never mind.

BEATRIZ. Let me get her.

AARON. No! Wait. Beatriz, listen. Deborah and I were talking. We thought … It's a bad time for us right now.

BEATRIZ. Pay me the basic respect. Don't talk to me about your marriage.

AARON. It's about Olivia.

BEATRIZ. I'm listening.

AARON. I think. Maybe it's better. Maybe Olivia should stay with you.

BEATRIZ. For the week?

AARON. Or maybe for the year. If you'll take her.

BEATRIZ. "If I'll take her."

AARON. I know it's a lot to ask. This environment … it's not healthy right now. *(Pause.)*

BEATRIZ. After all you put me through … I'll be damned.

AARON. Beatriz.

BEATRIZ. Telling the judge I was an unfit mother.

AARON. I'm not proud of how things went.

BEATRIZ. You said I couldn't read or write in English. You said my sister was an addict, that I was dating a slumlord.

AARON. Oh come on, I did not say that.

BEATRIZ. You and Deborah were going to raise my daughter "the right way."

AARON. We agreed, the decision was up to Olivia.

BEATRIZ. You agreed! A six-year-old can't make decisions like that.

AARON. The judge asked her, which parent do you want to stay with?

BEATRIZ. *Ay,* he wasn't going to let no white girl stay with Chiquita fucking banana!

AARON. The judge asked her, which parent do you want to go with and she said me, Beatriz. She pointed to me. *(Silence.)* Look, Deborah thinks it's better if—

BEATRIZ. Boy, she really steers the ship around there, doesn't she?

AARON. I think it's better if Olivia doesn't come back home —

35

BEATRIZ. Aaron! Of course I'll take her! It's the best thing you've ever given me.

AARON. Thank you. Tell her I said ...

BEATRIZ. Goodbye, Aaron. *(Beatriz hangs up. The shower stops. Olivia shouts from the bathroom.)*

OLIVIA. *(Offstage.)* Woo! That water was like a jackhammer, like Niagara Falls! Who were you talking to?

BEATRIZ. *(Shouts.)* I, uh, I was ordering a pizza ...

## Scene 14

*The motel room, late at night. Beatriz is asleep. Olivia sits by the window, writing. Moonlit mountains in the distance.*

OLIVIA. Four in the morning. *(Beatriz snores.)* Couldn't sleep. *Mountains. Montañas.* You see them in the distance, these blurry peaks. Where do they come from? Tremendous forces under the earth, altering the earth's surface. Plate tectonics. From Greek *tekton.* "One who constructs and destroys." Earth, land, divided into a number of vast, rigid plates. Plates shift one centimeter a year, they collide slowly. Mom and me and Dad and Deborah. We're all plates. Shifting, eliding, colliding, trying to fit together like jigsaw pieces, searching for the compatible edges. Trying to lock in. But something in us, plates of rigid land. Pieces that don't interlock. Trying to come together but making mountains instead. One centimeter here, one centimeter there until you're green and alive in places, covered in snow in others. Note, what kind of mountain will I be? Mom's definitely volcanic. Dad, he's more underwater mountain. Note — *(A reader appears in distant silhouette.)*

READER 2. Do I believe in true love?

OLIVIA. Note —

READER 2. If not, is that necessarily pessimistic? *(The motel phone rings. The reader disappears. Olivia answers the phone. Lights up on Manuel in Philadelphia.)*

OLIVIA. Hello?

MANUEL. Hi. I just got your message.

OLIVIA. Dad? Hey, Dad! How are you?

MANUEL. Olivia! *Ay, perdón,* it's Manuel. You sound all grown up.

OLIVIA. It's four in the morning.

MANUEL. How are you?

OLIVIA. Fine. How are you?

MANUEL. Ah, well, you know, I'm still here. My hair's going gray.

OLIVIA. It was gray the last time I saw you. Grandma's funeral.

MANUEL. What can you do? It's salt and pepper.

OLIVIA. Sorry we stole your car.

MANUEL. Nah, I've been taking taxis. So what did you do today?

OLIVIA. Mom taught me to dance. Well, she tried.

MANUEL. Did she lead?

OLIVIA. Yeah.

MANUEL. She always has to lead.

OLIVIA. How's business?

MANUEL. Up and down.

OLIVIA. What do you do again?

MANUEL. Contracting.

OLIVIA. Same as my dad.

MANUEL. On a larger scale.

OLIVIA. Mom's asleep. Should I wake her?

MANUEL. No, just have her call me in the morning. Or. Tell your mother I love her, okay?

OLIVIA. Okay.

MANUEL. Tell her I'm sorry.

OLIVIA. Sure …

MANUEL. Or, you don't have to. Never mind.

OLIVIA. Whatever you want …

MANUEL. Okay, let her know I took care of all the bills. And … I'm sorry.

OLIVIA. Okay.

MANUEL. She's been feeling alright?

OLIVIA. Yeah.

MANUEL. Good … I guess that's it. *(They hang up.)*

# Scene 15

*The Badlands. Beatriz and Olivia halfway up a mountain.
The mountain is the staircase. Beatriz pulls sandwiches out of
a bag. Olivia writes in her journal.*

OLIVIA. *(Writing.)* All those shadows.

BEATRIZ. Turkey cobb or egg salad?

OLIVIA. *(Writing.)* It looks like an old woman's scattered bones.

BEATRIZ. One day I'll be an old woman and I won't have to put
up with anyone else's bullshit. I'm taking the turkey.

OLIVIA. *(Writing.)* Erosion is so sad. They should call it the
Sadlands.

BEATRIZ. It's not sad or happy. It just is.

OLIVIA. *(Writing.)* Losing all your limbs, millimeter by millimeter, year after year, until you're scars, wrinkles, negative space.
*(Olivia finishes writing, puts her notebook away.)* Can we eat in the
car? That rest stop had a payphone. I want to call Dad before we
hit the road.

BEATRIZ. Ay, enough with the phone calls already. You know
what? No more quarters.

OLIVIA. Dad gets lonely if we don't talk.

BEATRIZ. You haven't spoken to him once.

OLIVIA. That's not true.

BEATRIZ. I read your notebook. *(A moment between the two.)*

OLIVIA. You have no right.

BEATRIZ. I thought you were pregnant.

OLIVIA. Wow. It's just really weird because you haven't read any
of my magazines. So I figured you weren't interested in my writing.

BEATRIZ. I was looking for anything, a clue.

OLIVIA. And it's also weird because if you want to know what's
going on in my life you can pick up the phone, dial a number and
ask me, "How are you doing, Olivia? How was your day today?"

BEATRIZ. This month has been extremely difficult. I know I've
been a stranger —

OLIVIA. Five months. You called me on my birthday, 9:30 at

night. That's the last time we spoke. I keep a log, I've kept it for three years. You want to know the exact number? How many times have you called me in the last three years?

BEATRIZ. Olivia, I go to sleep every night wishing I could talk to you!

OLIVIA. Then what is so hard about dialing seven numbers on a frickin' telephone? You want to know what's in my head? Why didn't you fight for me? *(Pause.)* The woman who screams and yells In court, you just sat there, you were so polite. You were quiet.

BEATRIZ. Is that what Aaron told you?

OLIVIA. I was there, Mom.

BEATRIZ. A lot happened behind closed doors. Aaron had his own way of fighting. He hit below the belt.

OLIVIA. But he fought for me.

BEATRIZ. I wasn't an American citizen, Olivia. And your father held it over my head! If they had deported me, would that make you happy?

OLIVIA. After you became a citizen, did you fight then? You moved on and so did I.

BEATRIZ. I have this one picture of me, four months after I lost you. You can see all my ribs. You can count each one. I couldn't get out of bed. I couldn't eat. I lost fifty pounds. My spine was like those rocks. *(Pause.)* I tried to kill myself.

OLIVIA. Mom …

BEATRIZ. Boo-fucking-hoo. I was dead already.

OLIVIA. How?

BEATRIZ. I swallowed six Nytols.

OLIVIA. So you didn't really want to die.

BEATRIZ. Then I swallowed thirty Valium.

OLIVIA. What saved you?

BEATRIZ. Manuel was my boss. He took me to the hospital and told me to surrender. He said, "If it's in God's plan, she'll be yours again someday. All you can do right now is surrender." Our first night together was in the E.R. I moved back to *el barrio*. Got a cleansing from a *santero*. Started speaking in Spanish again. I cooked every dish my mother had ever made. Manuel would pick me up in his green Jaguar and take me dancing 'til the clubs shut down. Then we would drive to Geno's, get cheese steaks with onions, go to the Art Museum steps and watch the sunrise.

OLIVIA. I didn't want to die.

BEATRIZ. What do you mean?

OLIVIA. When I tried it.

BEATRIZ. Tried what? What?

OLIVIA. Sixteen ibuprofen.

BEATRIZ. Olivia!

OLIVIA. Pretty futile attempt. It's pathetic actually. The first one I swallowed I thought, why am I doing this? I don't want to die. And then I swallowed the next one and thought, wow, now I really don't want to die. At the last pill all I could think was how I really want to live. I want to live. Then the bottle was empty.

BEATRIZ. Oh my God. Why, *mija?*

OLIVIA. Because.

BEATRIZ. You tell me why!

OLIVIA. I had gone to school wearing these ugly sweatpants and this group of guys kept saying, "White trash, white trash." I was handing out my magazine in the cafeteria. One of the guys came up and grabbed my magazines so I looked one way and then another guy was behind me on the other side and he pulled down my pants and my underwear kind of came down too and everyone was there. I had my period. So.

BEATRIZ. Oh, *mija.*

OLIVIA. After school I was going to ask Dad for a pair of jeans 'cuz, hey, you can't pull them down. He was upstairs so I asked Deborah if I could come up and she said no.

BEATRIZ. What kind of twisted shit is this?

OLIVIA. I thought maybe you could buy me a pair and mail them to me, so I asked if I could call you. *(Explaining.)* It's long distance.

BEATRIZ. I don't care if you're in China, you collect-call me!

OLIVIA. I was like, "Can I call Mom?" and Deborah was like, "When you talk about your mother it makes me uncomfortable. Don't talk about her around me."

BEATRIZ. "It makes me uncomfortable." Fuck you, bitch!

OLIVIA. *(Laughs.)* Once the bottle was empty I just sat there like, is this it, am I dying? Then I got freaked out and called the poison control center. They said sixteen ibuprofen wasn't enough to kill me if I threw up immediately. So I tore through the medicine cabinet, swallowed ipecac syrup and started throwing up. Sixteen times. One time for every pill.

BEATRIZ. Sixteen times…?

OLIVIA. I called you at number fifteen.

BEATRIZ. *(Realizing.)* Olivia!

OLIVIA. You honked the horn after number sixteen.

BEATRIZ. *Coño*, why didn't you say something? Jesus, I would have taken you to a doctor. You can't just have those chemicals floating through your system!

OLIVIA. I knew you'd get mad.

BEATRIZ. Mad? For having a sensitive heart? For being depressed that they treat you like a worthless piece of shit over there?

OLIVIA. Dad doesn't.

BEATRIZ. *Ay*, you have no idea! Trust me, I know things you don't!

OLIVIA. You don't know everything.

BEATRIZ. *Niña*, face the music, that man doesn't give two shits about you —

OLIVIA. That's not true!

BEATRIZ. You're so damn smart that you can't see what's right in front of your face!

OLIVIA. He! Loves! Me!

BEATRIZ. Earth to Olivia!

OLIVIA. HE DOESN'T SMILE ANYMORE! HE DOESN'T LAUGH! REMEMBER HOW HE USED TO LAUGH? DID DAD USED TO LAUGH?

BEATRIZ. I used to laugh, too! *Carajo*, I don't have the LUXURY of feeling lonely! One day you'll understand.

OLIVIA. I hope not.

BEATRIZ. Pass me the water.

OLIVIA. It's right next to you.

BEATRIZ. You were right.

OLIVIA. About what?

BEATRIZ. I didn't want to die. *(Pause.)* I wish I could kill those guys at your school.

OLIVIA. Whatever.

BEATRIZ. Why would they call you white trash?

OLIVIA. That was a compliment compared to the other things they said.

BEATRIZ. You're not white.

OLIVIA. Whatever you say!

BEATRIZ. I'm serious.

OLIVIA. Look at me!

BEATRIZ. Tell them, "Excuse me, I'm actually *Cubana*."

OLIVIA. I can't speak Spanish. I live in Paoli and go to Sugartown

High. I don't even tan right.

BEATRIZ.  You may not understand this, *mija*, but my skin is yours. Whether anyone else sees, you wear the skin of your mother. You got poor cousins in *el barrio* who buy milk with food stamps, you got a grandfather who was full-blood Arawak Indian, and you got their skin, too. Long after I'm in the ground and crumbled to dust, you'll still be wearing it. There's nothing you can do to ever get rid of it, and you better NEVER apologize for it! Okay?

OLIVIA.  I won't.

BEATRIZ.  I used to apologize for it. You understand me? Okay?

OLIVIA.  Okay. *(Pause.)* Good.

BEATRIZ.  It's not good or bad. It's like erosion. That's just how it is.

OLIVIA.  No, for me, it's good.


## Scene 16


*A small public library. Olivia sits at a table, surrounded by books, taking notes.*


OLIVIA.  Quick notes. Convinced Mom to drop me at library while she looks at antiques down the street. Headache from microfiche, handwriting too slow. Naomi Uemura. *(Uemura appears in distant shadow, at the bottom of a mountain, strapping on climbing gear. The staircase is the mountain.)* Japanese. First person to reach North Pole alone. First person to raft down Amazon alone. Walked the length of Japan. Soloed Kilimanjaro, Mont Blanc. Last year, age 43, decides to solo Mt. McKinley — highest peak in North America, 20,000 feet. But how to survive steep cracks with no partner to rope onto? Uemura ties bamboo poles over his shoulders to span any crevasse. No tent, no fuel, too much weight, will sleep in snow caves, eat cold food.

February 4, begins ascent. *(Uemura begins to climb. A brisk, determined pace.)* Dear Reader, can you imagine it? *(An anonymous reader enters, rapt in the pages of* The Issue.*)* The extreme loneliness of the Arctic summit —

READER 2.  — frostbite —

OLIVIA.  — altitude sickness —

READER 2.  — the terrible silence of ice for days —

OLIVIA.  — weeks —

READER 2.  — the mortal lure of falling asleep in the snow. Snow blindness —

OLIVIA.  — the distant sound of avalanches —

READER 2.  — rubbing your hands with snow to ward off frostbite.

OLIVIA.  An ice-bound world. February 12, Uemura radios to base camp. Has reached summit. Temperature minus fifty Fahrenheit. Plants Japanese flag. *(Climbing slower now, Uemura reaches the top of the mountain.)*

READER 2.  February 13, blizzard, no radio contact.

OLIVIA.  February 15, may be temporarily stranded on mountain. *(Uemura's image fades slightly.)*

READER 2.  February 17, pilot spots Uemura on icy slope. Uemura waves, "everything OK" signal. Blizzard worsens.

OLIVIA.  February 21, clouds break. Evac plane and helicopter dispatched.

READER 2.  A discovery in the snow: Uemura's right snowshoe.

OLIVIA.  February 29, in an ice cave: Uemura's diary. Final entry reads,

READER 2/OLIVIA.  "I wish I could sleep in a warm sleeping bag."

OLIVIA.  March 9, Associated Press reports —

READER 2.  "Team halts search for climber." *(Uemura disappears into white.)*

OLIVIA.  Dear Reader, there he is, frozen in time, new hikers clamoring layers above his ice-bound body. They want to ascend, to push their limits, to peak out, but almost immediately they'll have to turn around, descend back to the world again. They think the climb is the hard part, but it's the descent that got him. *(Beatriz enters, holding a gift box.)*

BEATRIZ.  Guess what I found. *(Reader 1 disappears. Mt. McKinley is gone.)*

OLIVIA.  An old faucet.

BEATRIZ.  No.

OLIVIA.  A lead glass doorknob. *(Beatriz hands Olivia the box.)* Just don't turn me into one of those people who have a hundred ceramic pigs because everyone thinks they're a collector and they never even liked pigs to begin with. *(Olivia opens it and pulls out a pair of opera glasses.)* Old binoculars …

BEATRIZ. Opera glasses. From London, 1800s. Find the manufacturer stamp. Is it smooth or bumpy?
OLIVIA. *(Running her finger over the stamp in the brass.)* Bumpy.
BEATRIZ. Which means? *(Olivia shrugs.)* It's hand-dated. Which means? *(Olivia shrugs.)* It's an original! Your brain is an encyclopedia and you can't remember that?
OLIVIA. *(Not getting it.)* I've never even been to the opera.

## Scene 17

*Back in Paoli, late at night. Aaron sits at the top of the steps, holding the answering machine. He holds down a button until it beeps.*

AARON. Hi, you've reached the Jacobs household. Sorry we couldn't come to the phone — *(He presses the button to stop recording. He holds down the button again until it beeps, starts recording.)* Hi, you've reached Aaron Jacobs. Sorry I'm not in right now, but leave a message and I'll get back to you as soon as I can. Have a good one. *(He stops recording. He starts recording again.)* This is Aaron, sorry I missed your call. If this is Olivia, hey there, kid. I uh, I finished the cabinet. I carved your initials under the bottom drawer, like always. The buyer came to pick it up and gave me three hundred extra, how 'bout that? So this weekend I'll go to the mall and find those jeans you were asking for. I'll send them to your mom's. I started a new job, it's the roof of an old barn. Milled the shingles myself. Cedar. I'll uh, I'll drive you by it when I'm done, okay? Or I'll send you a photo. *(He stops recording. He starts recording again.)* Hey. I'm not in right now. Leave a message. *(He's done. He puts the answering machine down.)*

## Scene 18

*In the car. Olivia is behind the wheel.*

BEATRIZ. You're doing good! You're a natural.
OLIVIA. Can I speed up?
BEATRIZ. No. *(Olivia speeds up.)* I said no!
OLIVIA. Seventy-five!
BEATRIZ. *Coño,* girl, slow down! They could take my license!
OLIVIA. Come on, eighty!
BEATRIZ. I shouldn't have let you behind the wheel! Slow!
OLIVIA. Look at the houses! Front lawns, flying by! Cars, people! Inches, feet, miles, centimeters! Gone before you see them!
BEATRIZ. Okay, okay, *suave, niña. Suave!*
OLIVIA. Faces, ribbons! Minutes, seconds! Look at those trees!
BEATRIZ. You slow the fuck down! *(Olivia slows down.)*
OLIVIA. *(Big, loud, a release.)* OKAY, I WAS TWELVE!
BEATRIZ. When you learned to drive?
OLIVIA. When I lost my virginity.
BEATRIZ. You lied to me!
OLIVIA. I watched the clock the whole time. It started at 4:50. Ended at 4:52.
BEATRIZ. If you had lived with me, you'd still be a virgin. I'd lock a chastity belt on you. Who was it?
OLIVIA. The guy who pulled down my pants in the caf.
BEATRIZ. That *hijo de puta!*
OLIVIA. That *hijo de puta!*
BEATRIZ. *(Making a game of it.)* OKAY, MANUEL CHEATED ON ME!
OLIVIA. What?
BEATRIZ. He got me good!
OLIVIA. I forgot, you were asleep and he called. A few nights ago. Holy crap, he said sorry.
BEATRIZ. Good, let him be scared. If he wants me back, let him beg. "*Ay, negra,* please!" Honestly, half the time *hombre* can't get it up!
OLIVIA. Ew.

BEATRIZ. I'm used to it, I'm an old pro. Your father wagged his matzo balls in every corner of our house, and not with me!
OLIVIA. No.
BEATRIZ. With Deborah.
OLIVIA. No! *(Pulls Beatriz's hair.)* You said the D-word.
BEATRIZ. Here's why I despise science fiction. You want to know why I can't stand science fiction?
OLIVIA. Why do you hate science fiction?
BEATRIZ. I tore through Aaron's study one day. Through every notebook, every journal. And then I noticed that *Hitchhiker's Guide to the Galaxy* looked very raggedy, so I pulled it off the shelf and out poured all of Deborah's love letters to him. Never trust a man who reads science fiction.
OLIVIA. Did you read them?
BEATRIZ. I still have them, if you want to see. That Christmas Aaron took me to Miller's Steak House, very expensive, the kind of place where they serve you a raw steak and it's supposed to be top of the line? I thought, *fíjate,* maybe he's going to choose me after all. He said, "BB, this Christmas I'm giving you the best gift of all." I said, *(Sings.)* *"Hit me with your best shot! Fire away!"* He said, "I'm giving you the gift of freedom. I'm leaving you."
OLIVIA. Jesus. I hate him.
BEATRIZ. No, you don't.
OLIVIA. I want to. I wish I could hate him. *(Pause.)* Does Manuel read science fiction, too?
BEATRIZ. *(Realizing the connection.)* Conspiracy books! Last month's phone bill. When I saw the amount, my eyes almost popped out of my head. There were hundreds of calls to the same number, so I dialed it. A woman answered. I said, "Good evening, this is the wife of Manuel Torres. With whom am I speaking?" She hung up. The next day I called and the number was disconnected.
OLIVIA. You said, "Good evening"?
BEATRIZ. I didn't know who I was calling.
OLIVIA. What did you say to Manuel?
BEATRIZ. Nothing, I just went to sleep. The next morning I made the coffee.
OLIVIA. That's it?
BEATRIZ. What did you expect, a parade?
OLIVIA. You told me to grow *cajones!*
BEATRIZ. *Co-jones.*

OLIVIA. Whatever.

BEATRIZ. *Cajones* means cardboard boxes. *Cojones* means balls.

OLIVIA. You should have said something. A simple, "How could you?" or "Get out!"

BEATRIZ. Words don't mean shit.

OLIVIA. You told me, take matters into your own hands.

BEATRIZ. *Carajo,* I should take my own advice. Where's your notebook?

OLIVIA. In my backpack. *(Beatriz pulls out Olivia's notebook, writes something, tears out the page, and tosses it out the window.)*

BEATRIZ. That's *my* Christmas present to him!

OLIVIA. What did you write?

BEATRIZ. Aaron Jacobs. *(Beatriz writes something on another piece of paper, rips it out.)* Manuel Torres! *(She tosses that paper out the window.)*

OLIVIA. Mom. *(Beatriz writes something on another piece of paper, rips it out, pauses.)* What does that one say? *(Beatriz doesn't answer.)* Mom? *(Beatriz puts that piece of paper inside her pocket. A sign appears in the distance.)* Oh shit.

BEATRIZ. What?

OLIVIA. Oh my God ... Mom ... AHHHHHH! *(Olivia laughs.)*

BEATRIZ. Don't scream like that when you're driving!

OLIVIA. Look at that sign!

BEATRIZ. You can read that? Where's my glasses?

OLIVIA. Oh my God ...

BEATRIZ. *(She finds her glasses, puts them on.)* I need better glasses ... Yellow ... Yellowstone?

OLIVIA. Breathe, Olivia ...

BEATRIZ. Uh, uh ... 16 West!

OLIVIA. Wait, do we want 16 East? Buffalo or Yellowstone?

BEATRIZ. Left lane!

OLIVIA. It says buffalo, right lane.

BEATRIZ. Get in the left lane!

OLIVIA. Ah!

BEATRIZ. Turn signal! *Coño!*

OLIVIA. Are you sure?

BEATRIZ. Exit! Use your mirrors!

OLIVIA. Okay, okay! My heart is racing.

BEATRIZ. Left. Left! Olivia! Visitors Center, that way!

OLIVIA. No, straight to the buffalo.

BEATRIZ. One thing at a time!

OLIVIA. Mom, I'm so happy.

BEATRIZ. You are?

OLIVIA. I'm so happy I want to cry. I'm sorry, we were talking about you and —

BEATRIZ. Seeing you happy, it's the only thing I need in life.

OLIVIA. Navigate. Hayden Valley. Look for it on the map. I'll keep my eye out for signs.

BEATRIZ. *(Looking at the map.)* Let's see. Soda Butt Creek.

OLIVIA. Butte.

BEATRIZ. That sounds nice.

OLIVIA. Hayden Valley, Mom, Hayden Valley!

BEATRIZ. Yellowstone Canyon Falls? You didn't tell me there were waterfalls here!

OLIVIA. No waterfalls!

BEATRIZ. Come on, I want to wash my face in a waterfall!

OLIVIA. You washed your face at the Motel 6!

BEATRIZ. That way to hot springs. Hot springs, *niña!* All those minerals, they're very healing. Please ...

OLIVIA. I feel like a kid who has to pee and the closer you get to home the more you have to pee. Ah! I'm going to explode! I saw it in two dimensions, and I'm going to see it in three dimensions! I'm going to see them!

BEATRIZ. Geysers? Old Faithful! Oh, come on! Are you going to stop your mother from seeing Old Faithful?

OLIVIA. On the way back! *(They pass some trees.)* Whoa, what is that?

BEATRIZ. Oh my God.

OLIVIA. There's no leaves. It's all white.

BEATRIZ. Ash. It looks like they burned it all. *(She reads a sign.)* "Forest regeneration ... fires ... "

OLIVIA. It looks like snow. Does it look like snow?

BEATRIZ. It looks like snow.

OLIVIA. The mountains are covered in snow. Mom. I can't steer, I can't see straight.

BEATRIZ. Both hands on the wheel!

OLIVIA. *Baja la ventana! Baja la ventana! (Beatriz lowers the window.)* I could fly away. I could fly right out of the window.

BEATRIZ. Watch the road. Stay in your lane.

OLIVIA. I could stampede. I could fly out the window and ... I could be ash. I could be a part of the river!

BEATRIZ. *(Seeing a sign.)* Hayden Valley! 26 miles!

OLIVIA. *(Seeing the sign.)* Oh my God. Mom, I don't know what to do. I don't know what to do. Help!

BEATRIZ. Twenty-six miles! You're getting close, *niña. Con calma.*

OLIVIA. Okay, breathe. Twenty-six miles. Twenty-six miles. Holy crap.

BEATRIZ. Calm down, Olivia. Don't get so crazy!

OLIVIA. How did you feel the day I was born?

BEATRIZ. *Ay dios mio,* what a question!

OLIVIA. Exactly, so just let me … Fly with me.

BEATRIZ. *Bueno.* I'm flying with you, okay?

OLIVIA. Hold my hand.

BEATRIZ. Two hands on the wheel.

OLIVIA. Hold my hand! *(Beatriz holds her hand.)*

BEATRIZ. Your pulse!

OLIVIA. I know.

BEATRIZ. Just breathe, okay? You're going to have a heart attack.

OLIVIA. *(Seeing another sign.)* Hayden Valley, 25 miles! *(Olivia spreads her arms, like to fly.)*

BEATRIZ. Keep your hands on the wheel! *(They seem to fly, soaring above the landscape.)*

OLIVIA. 24 miles!

BEATRIZ. 23!

OLIVIA. 22!

BEATRIZ. 21!

OLIVIA. 20! *(Fierce wind. They fly.)*

# Scene 19

*Hayden Valley. There are hundreds of buffalo scattered throughout the valley, off in the distance. Olivia and Beatriz sit on an overlook.*

*Olivia looks through the opera glasses.*

OLIVIA.  There's a mother and baby. *(Hands Beatriz the opera glasses.)*
BEATRIZ.  She's breastfeeding. *Ay que linda.*
OLIVIA.  I like the men. They butt heads.
BEATRIZ.  *(Puts the glasses down.)* Not a single person for three hours.
OLIVIA.  It's like the meadow has freckles. Slowly moving brown freckles.
BEATRIZ.  So this is it. *(Olivia finds her lucky magazine page in her backpack, holds it up against the actual landscape.)*
OLIVIA.  This is it.
BEATRIZ.  What next?
OLIVIA.  You get an image in your head. It feeds you. It keeps you breathing. Keeps your heart motivated to beat the next beat. Then, you see it.
BEATRIZ.  We could head back east. Highway it all the way back home.
OLIVIA.  Yeah.
BEATRIZ.  Keep going west. Find another diner. Another mountain. I'm in no rush. Just saying.
OLIVIA.  *(Looking out.)* It doesn't make you feel that there's any place to go. That there's clocks ticking anywhere. It just is.
BEATRIZ.  It just is. *(Pause.)* I'm pregnant.
OLIVIA.  Wow. Mom. Congratulations?
BEATRIZ.  I'm pregnant.
OLIVIA.  I'm going to be a sister. *(Beatriz doesn't respond.)* Does Manuel know?
BEATRIZ.  Yeah, he watched me pee on the stick.

OLIVIA. You'll figure it out. We'll figure it out.

BEATRIZ. That's sweet, Olivia.

OLIVIA. Is it a boy or girl?

BEATRIZ. I'm two months along. You don't find that out until later. *(Olivia puts her hand on her mother's belly. She closes her eyes.)*

OLIVIA. I think it's ... a girl. *(Beatriz holds Olivia's hand for a moment. A lifeline. Her only lifeline. And then, gently; she knows this will be rough.)*

BEATRIZ. I spoke with your father.

OLIVIA. When?

BEATRIZ. What would you think about staying with me for a while? In Philadelphia?

OLIVIA. Really? Like, next summer?

BEATRIZ. Or maybe this year.

OLIVIA. Hold on, is Dad okay?

BEATRIZ. He's fine.

OLIVIA. Why didn't you put me on the phone?

BEATRIZ. There's a room for you on the third floor. It has windows on three sides. You'd have your own bathroom.

OLIVIA. What did he say?

BEATRIZ. He and I both agreed. Move in for a month.

OLIVIA. He wants you to take me?

BEATRIZ. We can pick up your clothes on the way home.

OLIVIA. No ...

BEATRIZ. Move in for a week. You can stay at the same school, I'll drive you and pick you up.

OLIVIA. No way! Oh my God!

BEATRIZ. He doesn't want you back.

OLIVIA. Call Dad and tell him I said no!

BEATRIZ. I need your help. I can't do this on my own. I need a partner.

OLIVIA. Did you hear what I said?

BEATRIZ. *(About the buffalo picture.)* We can frame this and put it above your bedroom door. *(No response.)* Olivia, don't make me beg.

OLIVIA. *(Simply, with finality.)* I'm sorry. I'm not moving in with you.

BEATRIZ. *(Really asking.)* Why not? *(No answer.)* Say it to my face. Tell me, just like you told the judge.

OLIVIA. I was six, I don't remember.

BEATRIZ. Bullshit, you remember clear as day. Why your father? Why Aaron and not me? Look me in the eye and say the truth. "I'm more like Dad." That's what you said.

OLIVIA. I didn't mean it like that.

BEATRIZ. "I'm more like Dad." Say it.

OLIVIA. No.

BEATRIZ. *(Grabs Olivia's face toward hers.)* Dímelo!

OLIVIA. *(Softly.)* I'm more like Dad ...

BEATRIZ. *(Grabs her face violently.)* Hey! Look at me! I'm your mother so look me in the eye when you speak to me! And you better mean it this time!

OLIVIA. Ow!

BEATRIZ. Spit it out, Olivia! Say the words! Say the fucking truth!

OLIVIA. *(Looks her square in the eyes, shouts, primal.)* I'M! MORE! LIKE! DAD! *(Beatriz lets go of Olivia. Terrible silence. Then, the sound of buffalo hooves running in the distance. Both women look out. This is a quieter experience than either of them expected.)*

BEATRIZ. Did you feel that?

OLIVIA. Sound waves travel through the dirt more quickly ...

BEATRIZ. His hooves really touched the ground.

OLIVIA. I guess he wasn't flying after all. *(Pause.)*

BEATRIZ. My ass is killing me. Should we call it a day?

OLIVIA. The stars are coming out. Apparently they sizzle out here in September.

BEATRIZ. I'll go sit in the car for a minute. *(Hands Olivia her jacket.)* It's getting cold.

OLIVIA. Yup.

BEATRIZ. The wind is picking up.

OLIVIA. It is.

BEATRIZ. Take the jacket, please? *(Olivia doesn't. Beatriz leaves the jacket beside Olivia and exits. Olivia rips up her lucky magazine page.)*

# Scene 20

*Beatriz on a payphone. Aaron appears separately, in a hospital gown.*

AARON. You tracked me down, huh?

BEATRIZ. I called your house, Deborah gave me the number. Are you okay?

AARON. *(Downplaying it.)* I was putting in a roof, I lost my footing.

BEATRIZ. She said they kept you overnight.

AARON. *(Downplaying it.)* They try to be careful with concussions.

BEATRIZ. We're in Wyoming right now.

AARON. Oh. *(Realizing.)* Oh. I love Wyoming. All those parks. The Shoshone. The Grand Tetons.

BEATRIZ. Two days, Aaron, and I'm driving Olivia to your doorstep. I'm bringing her back to you.

AARON. Beatriz!

BEATRIZ. That's two days to get yourself together. To get you and that household ready for your daughter.

AARON. We had an agreement!

BEATRIZ. If you don't want Olivia, look her in the eye and tell her yourself. Drive her to Philadelphia yourself. Trust me, I'll take her any day of the week. You don't need to give me ten minutes notice. But my daughter will not be discarded! She will not be dropped on the side of the road! You will not quit your daughter! So you look in the mirror and tell yourself, "My daughter is coming home." Do you hear me?

AARON. Deborah gave me a week to pack my bags and go. *(Pause.)* You always believed in karma. *(Pause.)* What am I going to do, BB?

BEATRIZ. *(As a friend.)* You're going to hold on and I'm going to put your daughter on the phone.

# Scene 21

*The next day. In the car. Olivia reads* Changing Bodies, Changing Lives.

OLIVIA. "It's painful to have strong feelings for someone who doesn't return your affection. It's even more painful when you are still in love with someone who's no longer in love with you."
BEATRIZ. Can you find something less depressing in there?
OLIVIA. *(Turns the page.)* "Chapter 3: Exploring Sex with Yourself." *(Points.)* This is us.
BEATRIZ. East, huh?
OLIVIA. East ... *(And they turn in the direction of home.)*
BEATRIZ. You really won't tell me what your father said?
OLIVIA. "Sorry." He loves me. Blah blah. He'll never come out and say the one thing.
BEATRIZ. Which is?
OLIVIA. That it's easier to wake up in an empty house than one with me in it. *(Beatriz pulls a folded piece of paper out of her pocket.)* What's on the paper?
BEATRIZ. A name.
OLIVIA. Who's name?
BEATRIZ. Manuel's other ... The woman who picked up the phone. It shouldn't matter but it does. It matters, Olivia. *(Olivia takes the paper, opens it.)*
OLIVIA. "Susan McPhee"? *(A realization.)* She's white.
BEATRIZ. Like a piece of paper.
OLIVIA. *Ella es blanca. (Olivia ceremoniously throws the paper out the window. It spirals behind them. A moment. Then.)* You know what else I learned from *Changing Bodies, Changing Lives?*
BEATRIZ. I've created a monster.
OLIVIA. That teenagers can be Lamaze partners. *(They drive east.)*

# Scene 22

*Split scene.*

*In Paoli, Olivia sits at the typewriter.*

*In Philadelphia, Beatriz sits alone.*

OLIVIA. Dear Reader,
   What of the explorers who simply, plainly survive? Robert Capalio, an early South Pole researcher, described the Arctic landscape in scientific, stunning detail. And yet, most vivid is what he said about London when he returned home. "Oh, miracle of brick! Shiny black doors with brass knobs! Cars with spinning wheels! Oh, London, machine of joy, you are a cripple healed, standing anew, like the cured servant in Luke!" *(In Philadelphia, Manuel enters with a cup of coffee and hands Beatriz the cup. She drinks. In Paoli, Aaron enters, unseen, watches Olivia.)* Well, I'd never cracked open the Good Book until yesterday, when I stole a Bible from the Owl's Nest Motor Inn. Luke, Chapter 7, Verse 10: "And they that were sent, returning to the house, found the servant whole that had been sick." Dear Reader, do I believe in miracles? *(In Philadelphia, Manuel touches Beatriz's stomach.)* Your Founding Editor-in-Chief, Olivia *Cruz* Jacobs. *(She pulls the sheet from the typewriter, puts it in her notebook.)*
AARON. The car's all packed. What time is your mother expecting you?
OLIVIA. Today. No specific time.
AARON. You taking the typewriter with you?
OLIVIA. Mom's gonna buy me an electric one. They have ones that can erase now.
AARON. Nothing like a manual.
OLIVIA. You saved all my answering machine messages.
AARON. *(Nods.)* Did you check out the cedar planks in the garage?
OLIVIA. They smell incredible.
AARON. It looks like this studio apartment's going to work out

for me. Above the Chevy dealership on Route 30. Comes with a garage, so I can move my workshop there. *(Pause.)* For what it's worth. *(He hands Olivia a plastic bag. She pulls out a pair of jeans.)*
OLIVIA.   Cool. *(She hands her notebook to her father, like a gift. And also, like a goodbye.)* I made it to Wyoming.

## End of Play

# PROPERTY LIST

Magazine
Two wallets
Plastic bag
Book
Car keys
Folded-up magazine page
Banana
Cash
Map
Notebook, pen
Shopping bags with books, glass doorknob
Cassette tapes
Toothbrush
Purse with pregnancy test in plastic bag
Journal
Eyeglasses
Quarters
Tamales
Bag of sandwiches
Books
Climbing gear
Gift box with opera glasses
Answering machine
Backpack
Typewriter
Cup of coffee
Plastic bag with jeans

# SOUND EFFECTS

Phone rings
Car horn
Screen door slamming shut
Urinating, toilet flushing
Shower
Answering machine
Buffalo running

# NEW PLAYS

★ **YELLOW FACE by David Henry Hwang.** Asian-American playwright DHH leads a protest against the casting of Jonathan Pryce as the Eurasian pimp in the original Broadway production of *Miss Saigon*, condemning the practice as "yellowface." The lines between truth and fiction blur with hilarious and moving results in this unreliable memoir. "A pungent play of ideas with a big heart." –*Variety.* "Fabulously inventive." –*The New Yorker.* [5M, 2W] ISBN: 978-0-8222-2301-6

★ **33 VARIATIONS by Moisés Kaufmann.** A mother coming to terms with her daughter. A composer coming to terms with his genius. And, even though they're separated by 200 years, these two people share an obsession that might, even just for a moment, make time stand still. "A compellingly original and thoroughly watchable play for today." –*Talkin' Broadway.* [4M, 4W] ISBN: 978-0-8222-2392-4

★ **BOOM by Peter Sinn Nachtrieb.** A grad student's online personal ad lures a mysterious journalism student to his subterranean research lab. But when a major catastrophic event strikes the planet, their date takes on evolutionary significance and the fate of humanity hangs in the balance. "Darkly funny dialogue." –*NY Times.* "Literate, coarse, thoughtful, sweet, scabrously inappropriate." –*Washington City Paper.* [1M, 2W] ISBN: 978-0-8222-2370-2

★ **LOVE, LOSS AND WHAT I WORE by Nora Ephron and Delia Ephron, based on the book by Ilene Beckerman.** A play of monologues and ensemble pieces about women, clothes and memory covering all the important subjects—mothers, prom dresses, mothers, buying bras, mothers, hating purses and why we only wear black. "Funny, compelling." –*NY Times.* "So funny and so powerful." –*WowOwow.com.* [5W] ISBN: 978-0-8222-2355-9

★ **CIRCLE MIRROR TRANSFORMATION by Annie Baker.** When four lost New Englanders enrolled in Marty's community center drama class experiment with harmless games, hearts are quietly torn apart, and tiny wars of epic proportions are waged and won. "Absorbing, unblinking and sharply funny." –*NY Times.* [2M, 3W] ISBN: 978-0-8222-2445-7

★ **BROKE-OLOGY by Nathan Louis Jackson.** The King family has weathered the hardships of life and survived with their love for each other intact. But when two brothers are called home to take care of their father, they find themselves strangely at odds. "Engaging dialogue." –*TheaterMania.com.* "Assured, bighearted." –*Time Out.* [3M, 1W] ISBN: 978-0-8222-2428-0

**DRAMATISTS PLAY SERVICE, INC.**
440 Park Avenue South, New York, NY 10016  212-683-8960  Fax 212-213-1539
postmaster@dramatists.com  www.dramatists.com

# NEW PLAYS

★ **A CIVIL WAR CHRISTMAS: AN AMERICAN MUSICAL CELEBRA-TION by Paula Vogel, music by Daryl Waters.** It's 1864, and Washington, D.C. is settling down to the coldest Christmas Eve in years. Intertwining many lives, this musical shows us that the gladness of one's heart is the best gift of all. "Boldly inventive theater, warm and affecting." *–Talkin' Broadway.* "Crisp strokes of dialogue." *–NY Times.* [12M, 5W] ISBN: 978-0-8222-2361-0

★ **SPEECH & DEBATE by Stephen Karam.** Three teenage misfits in Salem, Oregon discover they are linked by a sex scandal that's rocked their town. "Savvy comedy." *–Variety.* "Hilarious, cliché-free, and immensely entertaining." *–NY Times.* "A strong, rangy play." *–NY Newsday.* [2M, 2W] ISBN: 978-0-8222-2286-6

★ **DIVIDING THE ESTATE by Horton Foote.** Matriarch Stella Gordon is determined not to divide her 100-year-old Texas estate, despite her family's declining wealth and the looming financial crisis. But her three children have another plan. "Goes for laughs and succeeds." *–NY Daily News.* "The theatrical equivalent of a page-turner." *–Bloomberg.com.* [4M, 9W] ISBN: 978-0-8222-2398-6

★ **WHY TORTURE IS WRONG, AND THE PEOPLE WHO LOVE THEM by Christopher Durang.** Christopher Durang turns political humor upside down with this raucous and provocative satire about America's growing homeland "insecurity." "A smashing new play." *–NY Observer.* "You may laugh yourself silly." *–Bloomberg News.* [4M, 3W] ISBN: 978-0-8222-2401-3

★ **FIFTY WORDS by Michael Weller.** While their nine-year-old son is away for the night on his first sleepover, Adam and Jan have an evening alone together, beginning a suspenseful nightlong roller-coaster ride of revelation, rancor, passion and humor. "Mr. Weller is a bold and productive dramatist." *–NY Times.* [1M, 1W] ISBN: 978-0-8222-2348-1

★ **BECKY'S NEW CAR by Steven Dietz.** Becky Foster is caught in middle age, middle management and in a middling marriage—with no prospects for change on the horizon. Then one night a socially inept and grief-struck millionaire stumbles into the car dealership where Becky works. "Gently and consistently funny." *–Variety.* "Perfect blend of hilarious comedy and substantial weight." *–Broadway Hour.* [4M, 3W] ISBN: 978-0-8222-2393-1

**DRAMATISTS PLAY SERVICE, INC.**
440 Park Avenue South, New York, NY 10016  212-683-8960  Fax 212-213-1539
postmaster@dramatists.com  www.dramatists.com

# NEW PLAYS

★ **AT HOME AT THE ZOO by Edward Albee.** Edward Albee delves deeper into his play THE ZOO STORY by adding a first act, HOMELIFE, which precedes Peter's fateful meeting with Jerry on a park bench in Central Park. "An essential and heartening experience." *–NY Times.* "Darkly comic and thrilling." *–Time Out.* "Genuinely fascinating." *–Journal News.* [2M, 1W] ISBN: 978-0-8222-2317-7

★ **PASSING STRANGE book and lyrics by Stew, music by Stew and Heidi Rodewald, created in collaboration with Annie Dorsen.** A daring musical about a young bohemian that takes you from black middle-class America to Amsterdam, Berlin and beyond on a journey towards personal and artistic authenticity. "Fresh, exuberant, bracingly inventive, bitingly funny, and full of heart." *–NY Times.* "The freshest musical in town!" *–Wall Street Journal.* "Excellent songs and a vulnerable heart." *–Variety.* [4M, 3W] ISBN: 978-0-8222-2400-6

★ **REASONS TO BE PRETTY by Neil LaBute.** Greg really, truly adores his girlfriend, Steph. Unfortunately, he also thinks she has a few physical imperfections, and when he mentions them, all hell breaks loose. "Tight, tense and emotionally true." *–Time Magazine.* "Lively and compulsively watchable." *–The Record.* [2M, 2W] ISBN: 978-0-8222-2394-8

★ **OPUS by Michael Hollinger.** With only a few days to rehearse a grueling Beethoven masterpiece, a world-class string quartet struggles to prepare their highest-profile performance ever—a televised ceremony at the White House. "Intimate, intense and profoundly moving." *–Time Out.* "Worthy of scores of bravissimos." *–BroadwayWorld.com.* [4M, 1W] ISBN: 978-0-8222-2363-4

★ **BECKY SHAW by Gina Gionfriddo.** When an evening calculated to bring happiness takes a dark turn, crisis and comedy ensue in this wickedly funny play that asks what we owe the people we love and the strangers who land on our doorstep. "As engrossing as it is ferociously funny." *–NY Times.* "Gionfriddo is some kind of genius." *–Variety.* [2M, 3W] ISBN: 978-0-8222-2402-0

★ **KICKING A DEAD HORSE by Sam Shepard.** Hobart Struther's horse has just dropped dead. In an eighty-minute monologue, he discusses what path brought him here in the first place, the fate of his marriage, his career, politics and eventually the nature of the universe. "Deeply instinctual and intuitive." *–NY Times.* "The brilliance is in the infinite reverberations Shepard extracts from his simple metaphor." *–TheaterMania.* [1M, 1W] ISBN: 978-0-8222-2336-8

**DRAMATISTS PLAY SERVICE, INC.**
**440 Park Avenue South, New York, NY 10016  212-683-8960  Fax 212-213-1539**
postmaster@dramatists.com   www.dramatists.com

# NEW PLAYS

★ **AUGUST: OSAGE COUNTY by Tracy Letts.** WINNER OF THE 2008 PULITZER PRIZE AND TONY AWARD. When the large Weston family reunites after Dad disappears, their Oklahoma homestead explodes in a maelstrom of repressed truths and unsettling secrets. "Fiercely funny and bitingly sad." –*NY Times.* "Ferociously entertaining." –*Variety.* "A hugely ambitious, highly combustible saga." –*NY Daily News.* [6M, 7W] ISBN: 978-0-8222-2300-9

★ **RUINED by Lynn Nottage.** WINNER OF THE 2009 PULITZER PRIZE. Set in a small mining town in Democratic Republic of Congo, RUINED is a haunting, probing work about the resilience of the human spirit during times of war. "A full-immersion drama of shocking complexity and moral ambiguity." –*Variety.* "Sincere, passionate, courageous." –*Chicago Tribune.* [8M, 4W] ISBN: 978-0-8222-2390-0

★ **GOD OF CARNAGE by Yasmina Reza, translated by Christopher Hampton.** WINNER OF THE 2009 TONY AWARD. A playground altercation between boys brings together their Brooklyn parents, leaving the couples in tatters as the rum flows and tensions explode. "Satisfyingly primitive entertainment." –*NY Times.* "Elegant, acerbic, entertainingly fueled on pure bile." –*Variety.* [2M, 2W] ISBN: 978-0-8222-2399-3

★ **THE SEAFARER by Conor McPherson.** Sharky has returned to Dublin to look after his irascible, aging brother. Old drinking buddies Ivan and Nicky are holed up at the house too, hoping to play some cards. But with the arrival of a stranger from the distant past, the stakes are raised ever higher. "Dark and enthralling Christmas fable." –*NY Times.* "A timeless classic." –*Hollywood Reporter.* [5M] ISBN: 978-0-8222-2284-2

★ **THE NEW CENTURY by Paul Rudnick.** When the playwright is Paul Rudnick, expectations are geared for a play both hilarious and smart, and this provocative and outrageous comedy is no exception. "The one-liners fly like rockets." –*NY Times.* "The funniest playwright around." –*Journal News.* [2M, 3W] ISBN: 978-0-8222-2315-3

★ **SHIPWRECKED! AN ENTERTAINMENT—THE AMAZING ADVENTURES OF LOUIS DE ROUGEMONT (AS TOLD BY HIMSELF) by Donald Margulies.** The amazing story of bravery, survival and celebrity that left nineteenth-century England spellbound. Dare to be whisked away. "A deft, literate narrative." –*LA Times.* "Springs to life like a theatrical pop-up book." –*NY Times.* [2M, 1W] ISBN: 978-0-8222-2341-2

**DRAMATISTS PLAY SERVICE, INC.**
440 Park Avenue South, New York, NY 10016   212-683-8960   Fax 212-213-1539
postmaster@dramatists.com   www.dramatists.com